AWS Elemental MediaTailor User Guide

A catalogue record for this book is available from the Hong Kong Public Libraries.

Published in Hong Kong by Samurai Media Limited.

Email: info@samuraimedia.org

ISBN 9789888408139

Contents

What Is AWS Elemental MediaTailor?

AWS Elemental MediaTailor is a scalable ad insertion service that runs in the AWS Cloud. With AWS Elemental MediaTailor, you can serve targeted ads to viewers while maintaining broadcast quality in over-the-top (OTT) video applications.

AWS Elemental MediaTailor offers important advances over traditional ad-tracking systems: ads are better monetized, more consistent in video quality and resolution, and easier to manage across multi-platform environments. AWS Elemental MediaTailor simplifies your ad workflow by allowing all IP-connected devices to render ads in the same way as other content. The service also offers advanced tracking of ad views, which further increases the monetization of content.

AWS Elemental MediaTailor supports Apple HTTP Live Streaming (HLS) manifest manipulation. If you require support for MPEG-DASH, create a feature request case with AWS Support.

- Are You a First-Time User of AWS Elemental MediaTailor?
- Concepts and Terminology
- How AWS Elemental MediaTailor Works
- Features of AWS Elemental MediaTailor
- Related Services
- Accessing AWS Elemental MediaTailor
- Pricing for AWS Elemental MediaTailor
- Regions for AWS Elemental MediaTailor
- Stream Requirements

Are You a First-Time User of AWS Elemental MediaTailor?

If you are a first-time user of AWS Elemental MediaTailor, we recommend that you begin by reading the following sections:

- Concepts and Terminology

- How AWS Elemental MediaTailor Works

- Features of AWS Elemental MediaTailor

- Getting Started with AWS Elemental MediaTailor

Related Services

- **Amazon CloudFront** is a global content delivery network (CDN) service that securely delivers data and videos to your viewers. Use CloudFront to deliver content with the best possible performance. For more information about CloudFront, see the Amazon CloudFront website.

- **AWS Elemental MediaPackage** is a just-in-time packaging and origination service that customizes live video assets for distribution in a format that is compatible with the device that makes the request. Use AWS Elemental MediaPackage as an origin server to prepare content and add ad markers before sending streams to AWS Elemental MediaTailor. For more information about how AWS Elemental MediaTailor works with origin servers, see How AWS Elemental MediaTailor Works.

- **AWS Identity and Access Management (IAM)** is a web service that helps you securely control access to AWS resources for your users. Use IAM to control who can use your AWS resources (authentication) and what resources they can use in which ways (authorization). For more information, see Setting Up AWS Elemental MediaTailor.

Accessing AWS Elemental MediaTailor

You can access AWS Elemental MediaTailor using the service's console.

You must access your AWS account by providing credentials that verify that you have permissions to use the services.

To log in to the AWS Elemental MediaTailor console, use the following link: **https://console/.aws/.amazon/.com/mediatailor/home**/.

Pricing for AWS Elemental MediaTailor

As with other AWS products, there are no contracts or minimum commitments for using AWS Elemental MediaTailor. You are charged based your use of the service. For more information, see AWS Elemental MediaTailor Pricing.

Regions for AWS Elemental MediaTailor

To reduce data latency in your applications, AWS Elemental MediaTailor offers regional endpoints to make your requests. To view the list of regions in which AWS Elemental MediaTailor is available, see http://docs.aws.amazon.com/general/latest/gr/rande.html#mediatailor_region.

Stream Requirements

A video stream must meet the following requirements to work with AWS Elemental MediaTailor:

- Uses HLS (Apple HTTP Live Streaming)
- Uses live streaming or video-on-demand (VOD)
- Is accessible on the public internet and has a public IP address
- Contains ad markers in one of the formats described in Step 2: Prepare a Stream

Concepts and Terminology

Configuration
An object in AWS Elemental MediaTailor that you interact with. The configuration holds location information about the origin server and ad decision server (ADS). The configuration also holds endpoints that provide access points in and out of AWS Elemental MediaTailor.

Dynamic transcoding
A process that matches the ad quality and format to the primary video content when content is requested. Dynamic transcoding reduces storage requirements and ensures that playback seamlessly transitions between the ad and video content.

Manifest manipulation
The process of rewriting manifests from the origin server so that the manifests reference the appropriate ad and content fragments. Ads are determined by the VAST response from the ad decision server (ADS). As playback progresses, AWS Elemental MediaTailor performs ad insertion or ad replacement into the content stream.

VAST and VMAP
Video Ad Serving Template (VAST) and Video Multiple Ad Playlist (VMAP) are XML responses that the ADS sends to ad requests from AWS Elemental MediaTailor. The responses dictate what ads AWS Elemental MediaTailor inserts in the manifest. VMAP also includes timing for ad breaks. For more information about the logic behind AWS Elemental MediaTailor ad insertion, see Ad Behavior in AWS Elemental MediaTailor. For more information about how AWS Elemental MediaTailor works with VAST, see VAST.

How AWS Elemental MediaTailor Works

AWS Elemental MediaTailor serves personalized content to viewers while maintaining broadcast quality-of-service in over-the-top (OTT) applications.

The general AWS Elemental MediaTailor processing flow is as follows:

1. A player or content distribution network (CDN) such as Amazon CloudFront sends a request for live or video-on-demand (VOD) HLS content to AWS Elemental MediaTailor. The request includes parameters from the player that include information about the viewer. Later, the ad decision server (ADS) uses these parameters to determine which ads are included in the AWS Elemental MediaTailor response to the content request. The format of the request varies depending on whether you use server-side or client-side reporting to track how much of an ad the viewer watches.

   For information about how the requests differ between the two reporting methods, see Ad Tracking Reporting in AWS Elemental MediaTailor. For information about configuring the ad targeting parameters, see Dynamic Ad Variables in AWS Elemental MediaTailor.

2. AWS Elemental MediaTailor pulls the fully formed template manifest from the content origin server (such as AWS Elemental MediaPackage). This manifest includes ad markers so that AWS Elemental MediaTailor knows where to perform an ad insertion or ad replacement.

3. Additionally, AWS Elemental MediaTailor sends a request to the ad decision server (ADS), including the player parameters from the content request.

4. The ADS provides a VAST or VMAP response that includes the ads to be played back, based on viewer information gathered from the parameters that AWS Elemental MediaTailor passed through, and current ad campaigns.

5. AWS Elemental MediaTailor manipulates the manifest to include the URLs for the appropriate ads from the VAST or VMAP response. For the logic behind how ads are inserted, see Ad Behavior in AWS Elemental MediaTailor.

6. AWS Elemental MediaTailor provides the fully customized manifest to the requesting CDN or player.

7. As playback progresses, either AWS Elemental MediaTailor or the video player reports how much of an ad is played. By default, AWS Elemental MediaTailor uses server-side reporting, meaning that the service sends ad viewing reports to the ad tracking URL directly, with no input required from you. If you require more control, you can instead perform client-side ad reporting, where AWS Elemental MediaTailor proxies the ad tracking URL to the player for it to perform ad tracking activities.

8. As the player requests ad segments throughout content playback, if the ad is not already transcoded in a format that matches the video content, AWS Elemental MediaTailor transcodes the ad at the time of the ad segment request. If an ad is not already transcoded, the service doesn't present it for playback at the first request.

Mixed Content Requests

Content requests are mixed when some requests are sent over HTTPS, while others are sent over HTTP. Player requests for manifests and ad segments from AWS Elemental MediaTailor are always sent over HTTPS. If the origin server only accepts HTTP requests, playback might fail at the player. To avoid playback issues, do one of the following:

- Use an origin server that supports HTTPS requests.
- Use a content distribution network (CDN) to enforce HTTPS requests. For more information, see Using HTTPS in Amazon CloudFront.

Manifest Response Latency

A certain amount of latency is normal for AWS Elemental MediaTailor responses to manifests. Latency mainly occurs for these three reasons:

- Manifest processing latency – time for AWS Elemental MediaTailor to look up entries in databases, and to compute and produce manifests. Latency is usually less than 100 milliseconds.

- ADS latency – time it takes for the ADS to respond to the AWS Elemental MediaTailor request. Latency is variable, but AWS Elemental MediaTailor times out if the ADS hasn't sent a response in 1.5 seconds or less.

- Origin server latency – time it takes for the origin server to respond to the AWS Elemental MediaTailor request. Latency is variable, but AWS Elemental MediaTailor times out if the origin server hasn't sent a response in 2 seconds or less.

Features of AWS Elemental MediaTailor

AWS Elemental MediaTailor supports the following features:

Ad Tracking Reporting
AWS Elemental MediaTailor offers both server-side and client-side ad view reporting:

- For server-side reporting, the service sends reporting information to ad tracking URLs directly.

- For client-side reporting, the service provides the beacons for the downstream player or content distribution network (CDN) to call directly to the ad decision server (ADS) for reporting on how much of an ad that a viewer watches, in quartile percentages (25%, 50%, 75%, or 100%). For more information about setting up reporting, see Ad Tracking Reporting in AWS Elemental MediaTailor.

Audio
AWS Elemental MediaTailor supports multiple audio tracks. For more information, see Alternate Audio and Subtitles.

Content and Ad Continuity
AWS Elemental MediaTailor uses a transcoding service to ensure that ads and content have the same bit rate and resolution so that transitions are smooth throughout playback.

Personalized Content
AWS Elemental MediaTailor uses VAST or VMAP to pass through viewer information to the ad decision server (ADS), and in return receives targeted ads that are relevant for the viewer.

Setting Up AWS Elemental MediaTailor

Before you start using AWS Elemental MediaTailor, complete the following steps.

- Signing Up for AWS
- Creating an Admin IAM User
- Creating a Non-Admin IAM User

Signing Up for AWS

If you do not have an AWS account, use the following procedure to create one.

To sign up for AWS

1. Open https://aws.amazon.com/ and choose **Create an AWS Account**.

2. Follow the online instructions.

Creating an Admin IAM User

When you first create an AWS account, you begin with a single sign-in identity that has complete access to all AWS services and resources in the account. This identity is called the AWS account *root user* and is accessed by signing in with the email address and password that you used to create the account. We strongly recommend that you do not use the root user for your everyday tasks, even the administrative ones. Instead, adhere to the best practice of using the root user only to create your first IAM user. Then securely lock away the root user credentials and use them to perform only a few account and service management tasks.

In this procedure, you will use the AWS account root user to create your first IAM user. You will add this IAM user to an Administrators group, to ensure that you have access to all services and their resources in your account. The next time that you access your AWS account, you should sign in with the credentials for this IAM user.

To create users with limited permissions, see Creating a Non-Admin IAM User.

To create an IAM user for yourself and add the user to an Administrators group

1. Use your AWS account email address and password to sign in as the *AWS account root user* to the IAM console at https://console.aws.amazon.com/iam/. **Note**
   We strongly recommend that you adhere to the best practice of using the **Administrator** user below and securely lock away the root user credentials. Sign in as the root user only to perform a few account and service management tasks.

2. In the navigation pane of the console, choose **Users**, and then choose **Add user**.

3. For **User name**, type ** Administrator**.

4. Select the check box next to **AWS Management Console access**, select **Custom password**, and then type the new user's password in the text box. You can optionally select **Require password reset** to force the user to select a new password the next time the user signs in.

5. Choose **Next: Permissions**.

6. On the **Set permissions for user** page, choose **Add user to group**.

7. Choose **Create group**.

8. In the **Create group** dialog box, type ** Administrators**.

9. For **Filter**, choose **Job function**.

10. In the policy list, select the check box for ** AdministratorAccess**. Then choose **Create group**.

11. Back in the list of groups, select the check box for your new group. Choose **Refresh** if necessary to see the group in the list.

12. Choose **Next: Review** to see the list of group memberships to be added to the new user. When you are ready to proceed, choose **Create user**.

You can use this same process to create more groups and users, and to give your users access to your AWS account resources. To learn about using policies to restrict users' permissions to specific AWS resources, go to Access Management and Example Policies.

For information about creating users with limited permissions, see Creating a Non-Admin IAM User.

Creating a Non-Admin IAM User

Users in the Administrators group for an account have access to all AWS services and resources in that account. This section describes how to create users with permissions that are limited to AWS Elemental MediaTailor.

- Step 1: Create Policies
- Step 2: Create User Groups
- Step 3: Create Users

Step 1: Create Policies

Create two policies for AWS Elemental MediaTailor: one to provide read/write access, and one to provide read-only access. Perform these steps one time only for each policy.

To create policies for AWS Elemental MediaTailor

1. Sign in to the AWS Management Console and open the IAM console at https://console.aws.amazon.com/iam/.

2. Use your Administrator user credentials to sign in to the IAM console.

3. In the navigation pane of the console, choose **Policies**, and then choose **Create policy**.

4. Choose the **JSON** tab and paste the following policy:

```
 1 {
 2      "Version": "2012-10-17",
 3      "Statement": [
 4          {
 5              "Effect": "Allow",
 6              "Action": "mediatailor:*",
 7              "Resource": "*"
 8          }
 9      ]
10 }
```

This policy allows all actions on all resources in AWS Elemental MediaTailor.

5. Choose **Review policy**.

6. On the **Review policy** page, for **Name**, type **MediaTailorAllAccess**, and then choose **Create policy**.

7. On the **Policies** page, repeat the steps in this section to create a read-only policy. Use the following policy and call it **MediaTailorReadOnlyAccess**:

```
 1 {
 2      "Version": "2012-10-17",
 3      "Statement": [
 4          {
 5              "Effect": "Allow",
 6              "Action": [
 7                  "mediatailor:GetConfig",
 8                  "mediatailor:GetAllConfigs"
 9              ],
10              "Resource": "*"
11          }
12      ]
13 }
```

Step 2: Create User Groups

Create a user group for each of the policies that you created in step 1. This way, when you create additional users you can add the users to a group rather than attaching individual policies to each user.

To create groups for users who need access to AWS Elemental MediaTailor

1. In the navigation pane of the IAM console, choose **Groups**, and then choose **Create New Group**.

2. On the **Set Group Name** page, type a name for the group, such as **MediaTailorAdmins**. Choose **Next Step**.

3. On the **Attach Policy** page, for **Filter**, choose **Customer Managed**.

4. In the policy list, choose the **MediaTailorAllAccess** policy that you created.

5. On the **Review** page, verify that the correct policy is added to this group, and then choose **Create Group**.

6. On the **Groups** page, repeat the steps in this section to create a user group that has read-only permissions. In step 4, choose **MediaTailorReadOnlyAccess**.

Step 3: Create Users

Create IAM users for the individuals who require access to AWS Elemental MediaTailor, and add each user to the appropriate user group to ensure that they have the right level of permissions. If you already have users created, skip to step 6 to modify the permissions for the users.

To create users who can access AWS Elemental MediaTailor

1. In the navigation pane of the IAM console, choose **Users**, and then choose **Add user**.

2. For **User name**, type the name that the user will use to sign in to AWS Elemental MediaTailor.

3. Select the check box next to **AWS Management Console access**, select **Custom password**, and then type the new user's password in the box. You can optionally select **Require password reset** to force the user to create a password the next time the user signs in.

4. Choose **Next: Permissions**.

5. On the **Set permissions for user** page, choose **Add user to group**.

6. In the group list, choose the group with the appropriate attached policy. Remember that permissions levels are as follows:

   - The group with the **MediaTailorAllAccess** policy allows all actions on all resources in AWS Elemental MediaTailor.

   - The group with the **MediaTailorReadOnlyAccess** policy allows read-only rights for all resources in AWS Elemental MediaTailor.

7. Choose **Next: Review** to see the list of group memberships to be added to the new user. When you are ready to proceed, choose **Create user**.

Getting Started with AWS Elemental MediaTailor

This Getting Started tutorial shows you how to integrate AWS Elemental MediaTailor into your workflow, including how to create an AWS Elemental MediaTailor configuration that holds information about the origin server and ad decision server (ADS).

- Prerequisites
- Step 1: Access AWS Elemental MediaTailor
- Step 2: Prepare a Stream
- Step 3: Configure ADS Request URL and Query Parameters
- Step 4: Create a Configuration
- Step 5: Test the Configuration
- Step 6: Send the Playback Request to AWS Elemental MediaTailor
- (Optional) Step 7: Monitor AWS Elemental MediaTailor Activity
- Step 8: Clean Up

Prerequisites

Before you can use AWS Elemental MediaTailor, you need an AWS account and the appropriate permissions to access, view, and edit AWS Elemental MediaTailor configurations. Complete the steps in Setting Up AWS Elemental MediaTailor, and then return to this tutorial.

Step 1: Access AWS Elemental MediaTailor

Using your IAM credentials, sign in to the AWS Elemental MediaTailor console at **https://console/.aws/.amazon/.com/mediatailor/home**/.

Step 2: Prepare a Stream

Configure your origin server to produce appropriately formatted HLS manifests.

Manifests must satisfy the following requirements:

- Manifests must be live or video-on-demand (VOD).

- Manifests must be accessible on the public internet.

- For live content, manifests must contain markers to delineate ad breaks. This is optional for VOD content, which can use VMAP timeoffsets instead.

  The manifest file must have ad slots marked with one of the following:

  - **#EXT-X-CUE-OUT / #EXT-X-CUE-IN** (more common) with durations as shown in the following example:

  ```
  1 #EXT-X-CUE-OUT:60.00
  2 #EXT-X-CUE-IN
  ```

  - **#EXT-X-DATERANGE** (less common) with durations as shown in the following example:

  ```
  1 #EXT-X-DATERANGE:ID="",START-DATE="",DURATION=30.000,SCTE35-OUT=0xF
  2 #EXT-X-DATERANGE:ID="",START-DATE="",DURATION=30.000,SCTE35-OUT=0xF
  ```

  All fields shown for **#EXT-X-DATERANGE** are required.

The way that you configure the ad markers in the manifest influences whether ads are inserted in a stream or replace other fragments in the stream. For more information, see Ad Behavior in AWS Elemental MediaTailor.

- The master playlists in the manifests must follow the HLS specification documented at HTTP Live Streaming: Master Playlist Tags. In particular, `#EXT-X-STREAM-INF` must include the fields `RESOLUTION`, `BANDWIDTH`, and `CODEC`.

When the stream is configured, note the URL to its master playlist. You need the URL when you create the configuration in AWS Elemental MediaTailor, in a later step of this procedure.

Step 3: Configure ADS Request URL and Query Parameters

To determine the query parameters that the ad decision server (ADS) requires, generate an ad tag URL from the ADS. This URL acts as a template for requests to the ADS, and consists of the following:

- Static values
- AWS Elemental MediaTailor-generated values (denoted by `session` or `avail` query parameters)
- Player-generated values, obtained from the client application (denoted by `player_params.` query parameters)

Example

```
1 https://my.ads.com/ad?output=vast&content_id=12345678&playerSession=[session.id]&cust_params=[
    player_params.cust_params]
```

Where:

- **output** and **content_id** are static values
- **correlator** is a dynamic value provided by AWS Elemental MediaTailor
- **cust_params** are player-supplied dynamic values

The master manifest request from the player must have corresponding key-value pairs for all `player_params.` query parameters in the ADS request URL. For more information about configuring key-value pairs in the request to AWS Elemental MediaTailor, see Dynamic Ad Variables in AWS Elemental MediaTailor.

Enter the configured "template" URL when you create the origin server/ADS mapping in AWS Elemental MediaTailor (step 4).

Testing Purposes

You can use a static VAST response from your ADS for testing purposes. Ideally, the VAST response returns a mezzanine quality *.mp4 rendition that AWS Elemental MediaTailor can transcode upon receipt. If the response from the ADS contains multiple playback renditions, AWS Elemental MediaTailor picks the highest quality and resolution *.mp4 rendition and sends it to the transcoder.

Step 4: Create a Configuration

The AWS Elemental MediaTailor configuration holds mapping information for the origin server and ad decision server (ADS).

To create a configuration (console)

1. Open the AWS Elemental MediaTailor console at https://console.aws.amazon.com/mediatailor/.

2. On the **Configurations** page, choose **Create configuration**.

3. For **Configuration name**, type a unique name that describes the configuration. The name is the primary identifier for the configuration. The maximum length allowed is 512 characters.

4. For **Video content source**, type the URL prefix for the master playlist for this stream, minus the asset ID. For example, if the master playlist URL is `http://origin-server.com/a/master.m3u8`, you would type `http://origin-server.com/a/`. Alternatively, you can type a shorter prefix such as `http://origin -server.com` but the `/a/` must be included in the asset ID in the player request for content. The maximum length is 512 characters. **Note**
If your content origin uses HTTPS, its certificate must be from a well-known certificate authority (it cannot be a self-signed certificate). Otherwise, AWS Elemental MediaTailor fails to connect to the content origin and can't serve manifests in response to player requests.

5. For **Ad decision server**, type the URL for your ad decision server (ADS). This is either the URL with variables as described in Step 3: Configure ADS Request URL and Query Parameters, or the static VAST URL that you are using for testing purposes. The maximum length is 25000 characters. **Note**
If your ADS uses HTTPS, its certificate must be from a well-known certificate authority (it cannot be a self-signed certificate). The same also applies to mezzanine ad URLs returned by the ADS. Otherwise, AWS Elemental MediaTailor can't retrieve and stitch ads into the manifests from the content origin.

6. Choose **Create configuration**.

    AWS Elemental MediaTailor displays the new configuration on the **Configurations** page.

Step 5: Test the Configuration

After you save the configuration, test the stream using a URL in the following format:

```
playback-endpoint/v1/master/hashed-account-id/origin-id/assetID.m3u8
```

Where:

- *playback-endpoint* is the unique playback endpoint that AWS Elemental MediaTailor generated when the configuration was created:

```
https://bdaaeb4bd9114c088964e4063f849065.mediatailor.us-east-1.amazonaws.com
```

- *hashed-account-id* is your AWS account ID:

```
111122223333
```

- *origin-id* is the name that you gave when creating the configuration:

```
myOrigin
```

- *assetID.m3u8* is the name of the master playlist from the test stream, excluding the URL path elements that you gave when adding the origin server to the AWS Elemental MediaTailor configuration.

Using the values from the preceding examples, the full URL is the following:

```
https://bdaaeb4bd9114c088964e4063f849065.mediatailor.us-east-1.amazonaws.com/v1/master
    /111122223333/myOrigin/assetID.m3u8
```

You can test the stream using one of the following methods:

- As shown in the preceding example, type the URL in a standalone player.
- Test the stream in your own player environment.

Step 6: Send the Playback Request to AWS Elemental MediaTailor

Configure the downstream player or CDN to send playback requests to the configuration's playback endpoint provided from AWS Elemental MediaTailor. Any player-defined dynamic variables that you used in the ADS request URL (in step 3) must be defined in the manifest request from the player.

Example
If your template ADS URL is the following:

```
1 https://my.ads.com/ad?output=vast&content_id=12345678&playerSession=[session.id]&cust_params=[
      player_params.cust_params]
```

Then define `[player_params.cust_params]` in the player request by prefacing the key-value pair with `ads..`. AWS Elemental MediaTailor passes any parameters that aren't preceded with `ads.` to the origin server instead of the ADS.
The player request URL is some variation of this:

```
1 https://bdaaeb4bd9114c088964e4063f849065.mediatailor.us-east-1.amazonaws.com/v1/master
      /111122223333/myOrigin/assetId.m3u8?ads.cust_params=viewerinfo
```

When AWS Elemental MediaTailor receives the player request, it defines the player variables based on the information in the request. The resulting ADS request URL is some variation of this:

```
1 https://my.ads.com/ad?output=vast&content_id=12345678&playerSession=<filled_in_session_id>&
      cust_params=viewerinfo
```

For more information about configuring key-value pairs to pass to the ADS, see Dynamic Ad Variables in AWS Elemental MediaTailor.

(Optional) Step 7: Monitor AWS Elemental MediaTailor Activity

Use Amazon CloudWatch and Amazon CloudWatch Logs to track AWS Elemental MediaTailor activity, such as the counts of requests, errors, and ad breaks filled.

If this is your first time using CloudWatch with AWS Elemental MediaTailor, create an AWS Identity and Access Management (IAM) role to allow communication between the services.

To allow AWS Elemental MediaTailor access to CloudWatch (console)

1. Open the IAM console at https://console.aws.amazon.com/iam/.

2. In the navigation pane of the IAM console, choose **Roles**, and then choose **Create role**.

3. Choose the **Another AWS account** role type.

4. For **Account ID**, type your AWS account ID.

5. Select **Require external ID** and enter **midas**. This option automatically adds a condition to the trust policy that allows the service to assume the role only if the request includes the correct `sts:ExternalID`.

6. Choose **Next: Permissions**.

7. Add a permissions policy that specifies what actions this role can complete. Select from one of the following options and choose **Next: Review**:

   • **CloudWatchLogsFullAccess** to provide full access to Amazon CloudWatch Logs.

   • **CloudWatchFullAccess** to provide full access to Amazon CloudWatch.

8. For **Role name**, type **MediaTailorLogger**, and then choose **Create role**.

9. On the **Roles** page, select the role that you just created.

10. Edit the trust relationship to update the principal:

1. On the role's **Summary** page, choose the **Trust relationship** tab.

2. Choose **Edit trust relationship**.

3. In the policy document, change the principal to the AWS Elemental MediaTailor service. It should look like this:

```
1  "Principal": {
2     "Service": "mediatailor.amazonaws.com"
3  },
```

The entire policy should read as follows:

```
1  {
2    "Version": "2012-10-17",
3    "Statement": [
4      {
5        "Effect": "Allow",
6        "Principal": {
7          "Service": "mediatailor.amazonaws.com"
8        },
9        "Action": "sts:AssumeRole",
10       "Condition": {
11         "StringEquals": {
12           "sts:ExternalId": "Midas"
13         }
14       }
15     }
16   ]
17 }
```

4. Choose **Update Trust Policy**.

Step 8: Clean Up

To avoid extraneous charges, delete all unnecessary configurations.

To delete a configuration (console)

1. On the AWS Elemental MediaTailor **Configurations** page, do one of the following:

   - Choose the **Configuration name** for the configuration that you want to delete.

   - In the **Configuration name** column, choose the radio button, and then choose **Delete**.

2. In the **Delete configuration** confirmation box, type **Delete**, and then choose **Delete** again.

AWS Elemental MediaTailor removes the configuration.

AWS Elemental MediaTailor Manifest Handling

A manifest is the input to AWS Elemental MediaTailor from an upstream encoder. When AWS Elemental MediaTailor receives a request for content playback, it manipulates the manifest and adds personalized content, tailored for each viewing session. The following sections describe the expected general behaviors of AWS Elemental MediaTailor manifest handling. For information about ad handling and insertion, see Ad Behavior in AWS Elemental MediaTailor.

- Alternate Audio and Subtitles
- HLS .m3u8 Manifests

Alternate Audio and Subtitles

AWS Elemental MediaTailor supports input and output of multiple audio and WebVTT subtitle tracks. To learn how AWS Elemental MediaTailor handles these tracks, see the following sections.

- Alternate Audio Expected Behavior
- Subtitles Expected Behavior

Alternate Audio Expected Behavior

If your content contains alternate audio, AWS Elemental MediaTailor transcodes audio-only renditions of the ads to the alternate audio tracks for your content. This way, audio switching continues to work during ad breaks. The service always inserts the default audio from the ad and replicates it across your audio tracks during ad breaks.

The audio bit rate must be from 16 to 320 kHz for ad transcoding to succeed.

Subtitles Expected Behavior

Ad playback does not include subtitles. Instead, AWS Elemental MediaTailor inserts blank offsets for the webVTT sidecar files during ad breaks.

HLS .m3u8 Manifests

AWS Elemental MediaTailor supports HLS manifests (*.m3u8) for live streaming and video on demand (VOD). Ad markers such as SCTE-IN/OUT and CUE-IN/OUT indicate ad breaks. The duration of the ad breaks is determined by the value in the `EXT-X-CUE-OUT` tag or by `EXT-X-DATERANGE Duration`. When AWS Elemental MediaTailor encounters an ad break, it attempts ad insertion or replacement, based on the type of content. If there aren't enough ads to fill the duration, AWS Elemental MediaTailor displays the underlying content stream or the configured slate for the remainder of the ad break. For more information about HLS ad behavior based on content type (live or VOD), see Ad Behavior in AWS Elemental MediaTailor.

When AWS Elemental MediaTailor stitches in ads, it first checks to see if the ads returned in the VAST response of the ad decision server (ADS) have been transcoded. If an ad has been transcoded, AWS Elemental MediaTailor uses the ad in the ad break. If it hasn't been transcoded, AWS Elemental MediaTailor transcodes it and stores it for future use. If there are multiple ads in the VAST response, AWS Elemental MediaTailor evaluates them sequentially and attempts to fill in subsequent ad creatives if the ads are already transcoded. If no ads are transcoded yet, AWS Elemental MediaTailor plays the underlying content (or ad slate) instead of the ad.

- HLS Live Manifest Examples
- HLS Manifest Tag Handling

HLS Live Manifest Examples

The following example shows a valid live master playlist as input to AWS Elemental MediaTailor.

```
1  #EXTM3U
2  #EXT-X-VERSION:3
3  #EXT-X-STREAM-INF:BANDWIDTH=878612,RESOLUTION=640x360,CODECS="avc1.4D4029,mp4a.40.2"
4  scte35_1.m3u8
5  #EXT-X-STREAM-INF:BANDWIDTH=2628628,RESOLUTION=1280x720,CODECS="avc1.4D4029,mp4a.40.2"
6  scte35_2.m3u8
7  #EXT-X-STREAM-INF:BANDWIDTH=1128660,RESOLUTION=854x480,CODECS="avc1.4D4029,mp4a.40.2"
8  scte35_3.m3u8
```

The following example shows a media playlist as input to AWS Elemental MediaTailor. Note the EXT-X-CUE-OUT and EXT-X-CUE-IN tags describing ad break opportunities.

```
1  #EXTM3U
2  #EXT-X-VERSION:3
3  #EXT-X-TARGETDURATION:4
4  #EXT-X-MEDIA-SEQUENCE:6719391
5  #EXTINF:4.000,
6  scte35_3_6719391.ts?m=1492714662
7  #EXTINF:3.533,
8  scte35_3_6719392.ts?m=1492714662
9  #EXT-OATCLS-SCTE35:/DA1AAALkmP0AP/wFAXwAlXbf+//4dg/yP4AQItwAAEBAQAAhT3BsQ==
10 #EXT-X-CUE-OUT:47.000
11 #EXTINF:0.467,
12 scte35_3_6719393.ts?m=1492714662
13 #EXT-X-CUE-OUT-CONT:ElapsedTime=0.453,Duration=47.000,SCTE35=/DA1AAALkmP0AP/wFAXwAlXbf+//4dg/
       yP4AQItwAAEBAQAAhT3BsQ==
14 #EXTINF:4.000,
15 scte35_3_6719394.ts?m=1492714662
16 #EXT-X-CUE-OUT-CONT:ElapsedTime=4.453,Duration=47.000,SCTE35=/DA1AAALkmP0AP/wFAXwAlXbf+//4dg/
       yP4AQItwAAEBAQAAhT3BsQ==
17 #EXTINF:4.000,
18 scte35_3_6719395.ts?m=1492714662
19 #EXT-X-CUE-OUT-CONT:ElapsedTime=8.453,Duration=47.000,SCTE35=/DA1AAALkmP0AP/wFAXwAlXbf+//4dg/
       yP4AQItwAAEBAQAAhT3BsQ==
20 #EXTINF:4.000,
21 scte35_3_6719396.ts?m=1492714662
22 #EXT-X-CUE-OUT-CONT:ElapsedTime=12.453,Duration=47.000,SCTE35=/DA1AAALkmP0AP/wFAXwAlXbf+//4dg/
       yP4AQItwAAEBAQAAhT3BsQ==
23 #EXTINF:4.000,
24 scte35_3_6719397.ts?m=1492714662
25 #EXT-X-CUE-OUT-CONT:ElapsedTime=16.453,Duration=47.000,SCTE35=/DA1AAALkmP0AP/wFAXwAlXbf+//4dg/
       yP4AQItwAAEBAQAAhT3BsQ==
26 #EXTINF:4.000,
27 scte35_3_6719398.ts?m=1492714662
28 #EXT-X-CUE-OUT-CONT:ElapsedTime=20.453,Duration=47.000,SCTE35=/DA1AAALkmP0AP/wFAXwAlXbf+//4dg/
       yP4AQItwAAEBAQAAhT3BsQ==
29 #EXTINF:4.000,
30 scte35_3_6719399.ts?m=1492714662
31 #EXT-X-CUE-OUT-CONT:ElapsedTime=24.453,Duration=47.000,SCTE35=/DA1AAALkmP0AP/wFAXwAlXbf+//4dg/
       yP4AQItwAAEBAQAAhT3BsQ==
32 #EXTINF:4.000,
```

```
33  scte35_3_6719400.ts?m=1492714662
34  #EXT-X-CUE-OUT-CONT:ElapsedTime=28.453,Duration=47.000,SCTE35=/DAlAAALkmPOAP/wFAXwAlXbf+//4dg/
        yP4AQItwAAEBAQAAhT3BsQ==
35  #EXTINF:4.000,
36  scte35_3_6719401.ts?m=1492714662
37  #EXT-X-CUE-OUT-CONT:ElapsedTime=32.453,Duration=47.000,SCTE35=/DAlAAALkmPOAP/wFAXwAlXbf+//4dg/
        yP4AQItwAAEBAQAAhT3BsQ==
38  #EXTINF:4.000,
39  scte35_3_6719402.ts?m=1492714662
40  #EXT-X-CUE-OUT-CONT:ElapsedTime=36.453,Duration=47.000,SCTE35=/DAlAAALkmPOAP/wFAXwAlXbf+//4dg/
        yP4AQItwAAEBAQAAhT3BsQ==
41  #EXTINF:4.000,
42  scte35_3_6719403.ts?m=1492714662
43  #EXT-X-CUE-OUT-CONT:ElapsedTime=40.453,Duration=47.000,SCTE35=/DAlAAALkmPOAP/wFAXwAlXbf+//4dg/
        yP4AQItwAAEBAQAAhT3BsQ==
44  #EXTINF:4.000,
45  scte35_3_6719404.ts?m=1492714662
46  #EXT-X-CUE-OUT-CONT:ElapsedTime=44.453,Duration=47.000,SCTE35=/DAlAAALkmPOAP/wFAXwAlXbf+//4dg/
        yP4AQItwAAEBAQAAhT3BsQ==
47  #EXTINF:2.533,
48  scte35_3_6719405.ts?m=1492714662
49  #EXT-X-CUE-IN
50  #EXTINF:1.467,
51  scte35_3_6719406.ts?m=1492714662
```

HLS Manifest Tag Handling

AWS Elemental MediaTailor outputs all unknown and custom tags into the personalized output manifest with the exception of `EXT-X-CUE- OUT/IN` tags, whose handling is described below.

To work properly, AWS Elemental MediaTailor requires HLS `EXT-X-VERSION` 3 or higher as the input manifest.

- EXT-X-CUE Tags
- EXT-X-KEY Value

EXT-X-CUE Tags

AWS Elemental MediaTailor converts `EXT-X-CUE-OUT`, `EXT-X-CUE-OUT-CONT`, and `EXT-X-CUE-IN` tags from the input manifest to `EXT-X-DISCONTINUITY` tags in the output manifest to identify discrete ad creative boundaries. AWS Elemental MediaTailor inserts an `EXT-X-DISCONTINUITY` tag at the start and end of every ad, including the following boundaries:

- Where content transitions to an ad

- Where one ad transitions to another ad

- Where an ad transitions back to content

EXT-X-KEY Value

If the origin server has enabled encryption or digital rights management (DRM) on the content stream, the manifest includes `EXT-X-KEY` tags. Because ads aren't encrypted, AWS Elemental MediaTailor sets the `EXT-X-KEY` tag to `NONE` for ad breaks. When playback returns to the content stream, AWS Elemental MediaTailor re-enables the `EXT-X-KEY` tag.

Working with Configurations in AWS Elemental MediaTailor

A configuration is an object that you interact with in AWS Elemental MediaTailor. The configuration holds the mapping information for the origin server and the ad decision server (ADS). You can also define what the playback defaults to if an ad isn't available or doesn't fill the entire ad break.

If you are using a content distribution network (CDN) with AWS Elemental MediaTailor, you have to set up the behavior rules in the CDN before you add CDN information to the configuration. For more information about setting up your CDN, see Integrating AWS Elemental MediaTailor and a CDN.

- Creating a Configuration
- Viewing a Configuration
- Editing a Configuration
- Deleting a Configuration

Creating a Configuration

Create a configuration to start receiving content streams and to provide an access point for downstream playback devices to request content.

To add a configuration (console)

1. Open the AWS Elemental MediaTailor console at https://console.aws.amazon.com/mediatailor/.

2. On the **Configurations** page, choose **Create configuration**.

3. For **Configuration name**, type a unique name that describes the configuration. The name is the primary identifier for the configuration. The maximum length allowed is 512 characters.

4. For **Video content source**, type the URL prefix for the master playlist for this stream, minus the asset ID. For example, if the master playlist URL is `http://origin-server.com/a/master.m3u8`, you would type `http://origin-server.com/a/`. Alternatively, you can type a shorter prefix such as `http://origin-erver.com` but the `/a/` must be included in the asset ID in the player request for content. The maximum length is 512 characters. **Note**
If your content origin uses HTTPS, its certificate must be from a well-known certificate authority (it cannot be a self-signed certificate). Otherwise, AWS Elemental MediaTailor fails to connect to the content origin and can't serve manifests in response to player requests.

5. For **Ad decision server**, type the URL for your ad decision server (ADS). This is either the URL with variables as described in Step 3: Configure ADS Request URL and Query Parameters, or the static VAST URL that you are using for testing purposes. The maximum length is 25000 characters. **Note**
If your ADS uses HTTPS, its certificate must be from a well-known certificate authority (it cannot be a self-signed certificate). The same also applies to mezzanine ad URLs returned by the ADS. Otherwise, AWS Elemental MediaTailor can't retrieve and stitch ads into the manifests from the content origin.

6. For **Slate ad**, type the URL for a high-quality MP4 asset to transcode and use to fill in time that's not used by ads. AWS Elemental MediaTailor shows the slate to fill in gaps in media content. Configuring the slate is optional for non-VPAID configurations. For VPAID, you must configure a slate, which AWS Elemental MediaTailor provides in the slots designated for dynamic ad content. The slate must be a high-quality MP4 asset that contains both audio and video. For more information, see Slate Management .
Note
If the server that hosts your slate uses HTTPS, its certificate must be from a well-known certificate authority (it cannot be a self-signed certificate). Otherwise, AWS Elemental MediaTailor can't retrieve and stitch the slate into the manifests from the content origin.

7. (Optional) The **CDN content segment prefix** enables AWS Elemental MediaTailor to create manifests with URLs to your CDN path for content segments. Before you do this step, set up a rule in your CDN to pull segments from your origin server. For **CDN content segment prefix**, type the CDN prefix path.

   For more information about integrating AWS Elemental MediaTailor with a CDN, see CDN Integration.

8. (Optional) The **CDN ad segment prefix** enables AWS Elemental MediaTailor to create manifests with URLs to your own CDN path for ad segments. By default, AWS Elemental MediaTailor serves ad segments from an internal Amazon CloudFront distribution with default cache settings. Before you can complete the **CDN ad segment prefix** field, you must set up a rule in your CDN to pull ad segments from the following origin:

   ```
   1 https://ad.mediatailor.<region>.amazonaws.com
   ```

   For **CDN ads segment prefix**, type the name of your CDN prefix in the configuration.

   For more information about integrating AWS Elemental MediaTailor with a CDN, see CDN Integration.

9. Choose **Create configuration**.

   AWS Elemental MediaTailor displays the new configuration in the table on the **Configurations** page.

10. (Optional, but recommended) You can use the configuration playback URLs to set up a CDN with AWS Elemental MediaTailor for manifests and reporting.

For information about setting up a CDN for manifest and reporting requests, see Integrating AWS Elemental MediaTailor and a CDN.

Viewing a Configuration

View the configuration's current settings.

To view a configuration

1. Open the AWS Elemental MediaTailor console at https://console.aws.amazon.com/mediatailor/.

2. On the **Configurations** page, choose the **Configuration name** for the configuration to view.

   In addition to the values provided when the configuration was created, AWS Elemental MediaTailor displays the name of the configuration, playback endpoints, and relevant access URLs.

Editing a Configuration

Edit a configuration to update the origin server and ad decision server (ADS) mapping, or change how AWS Elemental MediaTailor interacts with a content distribution network (CDN).

**To edit a configuration **

1. Open the AWS Elemental MediaTailor console at https://console.aws.amazon.com/mediatailor/.

2. On the **Configurations** page, choose the name of the configuration that you want to edit.

3. On the configuration details page, choose **Edit**, and then revise the configuration settings as needed. Note that you can't edit the configuration name. For information about configuration attributes, see Creating a Configuration.

4. Choose **Save**.

Deleting a Configuration

Delete a configuration to make it unavailable for playback.

To delete a configuration

1. Open the AWS Elemental MediaTailor console at https://console.aws.amazon.com/mediatailor/.

2. On the **Configurations** page, do one of the following:

   - Choose the name of the configuration that you want to delete.

   - In the **Configuration name** column, choose the radio button, and then choose **Delete**.

3. In the **Delete** confirmation box, type **Delete**, and then choose **Delete**.

Integrating with AWS Elemental MediaTailor

This section describes optional integrations with AWS Elemental MediaTailor that you can perform to optimize your manifest personalization experience.

- CDN Integration

CDN Integration

We highly recommend that you use a content distribution network (CDN) such as Amazon CloudFront to improve the efficiency of the ad stitching workflow between AWS Elemental MediaTailor and your users. The benefits of a CDN include content and ad caching, consistent domain names across personalized manifests, and CDN DNS resolution.

When you use a CDN in the AWS Elemental MediaTailor workflow, the request and response flow is as follows:

1. The player requests a master manifest from the CDN with AWS Elemental MediaTailor as the manifest origin. Personalized manifest requests are proxied through the CDN, and the CDN forwards the requests to AWS Elemental MediaTailor.

2. AWS Elemental MediaTailor personalizes the manifest and substitutes CDN domain names for the content and ad segment URL prefixes. AWS Elemental MediaTailor sends the personalized manifest as a response to the CDN and consequently to the requesting player.

3. The player requests segments from the URLs that are provided in the master manifest.

4. The CDN translates the segment URLs and forwards content segment requests to the origin server and ad requests to the Amazon CloudFront distribution where AWS Elemental MediaTailor stores transcoded ads.

5. The origin server and AWS Elemental MediaTailor respond with the requested segments, and playback begins.

The following sections describe how to configure AWS Elemental MediaTailor and the CDN to perform this flow.

- Integrating AWS Elemental MediaTailor and a CDN

Integrating AWS Elemental MediaTailor and a CDN

The following steps show how to integrate AWS Elemental MediaTailor with your content distribution network (CDN). Depending on the CDN that you use, some terminology might differ from what is used in these steps.

Step 1: (CDN) Create Routing Behaviors

In the CDN, create behaviors and rules that route content segment requests to the origin server and ad segment requests to AWS Elemental MediaTailor, as follows:

- Create one behavior that routes *content segment* requests to the *origin server * based on a rule that includes a phrase to differentiate content segment requests from ad segment requests.

  For example, the CDN routes player requests to `https://CDN_Hostname/subdir/content.ts` to the origin server path `http://origin.com/contentpath/subdir/content.ts` based on the keyword **subdir** in the request.

- Create one behavior that routes *ad segment* requests to the internal Amazon CloudFront distribution where AWS Elemental MediaTailor stores transcoded ads, based on a rule that includes a phrase to differentiate ad segment requests from content segment requests.

  These are the default Amazon CloudFront distributions that AWS Elemental MediaTailor uses for storing ads:

  - `https://ads.mediatailor.us-east-1.amazonaws.com`
  - `https://ads.mediatailor.eu-west-1.amazonaws.com`

  This step is optional because AWS Elemental MediaTailor provides a default CDN configuration for ad serving.

Step 2: (AWS Elemental MediaTailor) Create a Configuration with CDN Mapping

Create an AWS Elemental MediaTailor configuration that maps the domains of the CDN routing behaviors to the origin server and to the location where the ads are stored. Type the domain names in the configuration as follows:

- For **CDN content segment prefix**, type the CDN domain from the behavior that you created to route content requests to the origin server. In the master manifest, AWS Elemental MediaTailor replaces the content segment URL prefix with the CDN domain.

  For example,

  - If the full content file path is `http://origin.com/contentpath/subdir/content.ts`,
  - then the **Video content source** in the AWS Elemental MediaTailor configuration is `http://origin.com/contentpath/`,
  - and the **CDN content segment prefix** is `https://CDN_Hostname/`,
  - then the content segment advertised in the master manifest that AWS Elemental MediaTailor serves is `https://CDN_Hostname/subdir/content.ts`.

- For **CDN ad segment prefix**, type the name of the CDN behavior that you created to route ad requests through your CDN. In the playlist manifest, AWS Elemental MediaTailor replaces the Amazon CloudFront distribution with the behavior name.

Step 3: (CDN) Set up CDN for Manifest and Reporting Requests

Using a CDN for manifest and reporting requests enables additional functionality in your workflow.

For manifests, referencing a CDN in front of `/v1/master` (in master playlist requests) or `/v1/manifest` (for manifest playlist requests) lets you use CDN features such as geofencing, and also lets you serve everything from your own domain name. For this path, do not cache the manifests because they are all personalized.

For reporting, referencing a CDN in front of `/v1/segment` in ad segment requests helps prevent AWS Elemental MediaTailor from sending duplicate ad tracking beacons. When a player makes a request for a /v1/segment ad, AWS Elemental MediaTailor issues a 301 redirect to the actual *.ts segment. When AWS Elemental MediaTailor sees that `/v1/segment` request, it issues a beacon call to track the view percentage of the ad. If the same player makes multiple requests for the same `/v1/segment` in one session, and your ADS can't de-duplicate requests, then AWS Elemental MediaTailor issues multiple requests for the same beacon. Using a CDN to cache these 301 responses ensures that AWS Elemental MediaTailor doesn't make duplicate beacon calls for repeated requests. For this path, you can use a high or default cache because cache-keys for these segments are unique.

To take advantage of these benefits, create behaviors in the CDN that route requests to the AWS Elemental MediaTailor configuration endpoint based on rules that differentiate requests for master manifests, media playlists, and reporting. Requests follow these formats:

- Master manifests: `https://<playback-endpoint>/v1/master/<hashed-account-id>/<origin-id>/<assetID>.m3u8`
  Example

  1 `https://a57b77e98569478b83c10881a22b7a24.mediatailor.us-east-1.amazonaws.com/v1/master/`
  `a1bc06b59e9a570b3b6b886a763d15814a86f0bb/Demo/assetId.m3u8`

- Media playlists: `https://<playback-endpoint>/v1/manifest/<hashed-account-id>/<session-id>/<playlistNumber>.m3u8`
  Example

  1 `https://a57b77e98569478b83c10881a22b7a24.mediatailor.us-east-1.amazonaws.com/v1/manifest/`
  `a1bc06b59e9a570b3b6b886a763d15814a86f0bb/c240ea66-9b07-4770-8ef9-7d16d916b407/0.m3u8`

- Ad reporting requests for server-side reporting: `https://<playback-endpoint>/v1/segment/<origin-id>/<session-id>/<playlistNum>/<HLSSequenceNum>`
  Example

  1 `https://a57b77e98569478b83c10881a22b7a24.mediatailor.us-east-1.amazonaws.com/v1/segment/`
  `Demo/240ea66-9b07-4770-8ef9-7d16d916b407/0/440384`

In the CDN, create a behavior that routes manifest requests to the AWS Elemental MediaTailor configuration endpoint based on a rule that includes a phrase to differentiate the manifest request from segment requests.

For example, player requests to `https://CDN_Hostname/some/path/asset.m3u8` are routed to the AWS Elemental MediaTailor path `https://mediatailor.us-west-2.amazonaws.com/v1/session/configuration/endpoint` based on the keyword ***.m3u8** in the request.

VAST

This topic covers the use of the Interactive Advertising Bureau (IAB) Video Ad Serving Template (VAST), Video Player Ad-Serving Interface Definition (VPAID), and Video Multiple Ad Playlist (VMAP).

AWS Elemental MediaTailor supports VAST 3.0 and 2.0 and VMAP 1.0 for server-side ad insertion. AWS Elemental MediaTailor also supports the proxying of VPAID metadata through our client-side reporting API, for client-side ad insertion. For information on client-side reporting, see Client-side Reporting.

For IAB specifications, see the following:

- VAST 3.0 – https://www.iab.com/guidelines/digital-video-ad-serving-template-vast-3-0/
- VMAP 1.0 – https://www.iab.com/guidelines/digital-video-multiple-ad-playlist-vmap-1-0-1/
- VPAID – https://www.iab.com/guidelines/digital-video-player-ad-interface-definition-vpaid-2-0/
- VAST Integration
- VPAID Handling

VAST Integration

To integrate your ad server with AWS Elemental MediaTailor, your ad server must send XML that conforms to the IAB specifications for the supported versions of VAST and VMAP. You can use a public VAST validator to ensure that these tags are well-formed.

Make sure that your ad server's VAST response contains IAB compliant `TrackingEvents` elements and standard event types like `impression`. If you don't include standard tracking events, AWS Elemental MediaTailor rejects the VAST response and doesn't provide an ad fill for the break.

VAST 3.0 introduced support for ad pods, which is the delivery of a set of sequential linear ads. With AWS Elemental MediaTailor if a specific ad in an ad pod is not available, AWS Elemental MediaTailor logs an error on CloudWatch, in the interactions log of the ad decision servers, and tries to insert the next ad in the pod. In this way, AWS Elemental MediaTailor iterates through the ads in the pod until it finds one that it can use.

Targeting

To target specific players for your ads, you can create templates for your ad tags and URLs. For more information, see Dynamic Ad Variables in AWS Elemental MediaTailor.

AWS Elemental MediaTailor proxies the player's `user-agent` and `x-forwarded-for` headers when it sends the ad server VAST request and when it makes the server-side tracking calls. Make sure that your ad server can handle these headers. Alternatively, you can use `[session.user_agent]` or `[session.client_ip]` and pass these values in query strings on the ad tag and ad URL. For more information, see Session Data.

Ad Calls

AWS Elemental MediaTailor calls your VAST ads URL as defined in your configuration, substituting any player-specific or session-specific parameters when making the ad call. AWS Elemental MediaTailor follows up to three levels of VAST wrappers and redirects in the VAST response. In live streaming scenarios, AWS Elemental MediaTailor makes ad calls simultaneously at ad break start for connected players. In practice, due to jitter, these ad calls can be spread out over a few seconds. Make sure that your ad server can handle the number of concurrent connections this type of calling requires. AWS Elemental MediaTailor does not currently support pre-fetching VAST responses.

Creative Handling

When AWS Elemental MediaTailor receives the ADS VAST response, for each creative it identifies the highest bit rate `MediaFile` for transcoding and uses this as its source. It sends this file to the on-the-fly transcoder for transformation into renditions that fit the player's master manifest bit rates and resolutions. For best results, make sure that your highest bit rate media file is a high-quality MP4 asset with valid manifest presets. When manifest presets are not valid, the transcode jobs fail, resulting in no ad shown. Examples of presets that are not valid include unsupported input file formats, like ProRes, and certain rendition specifications, like the resolution 855X481.

Creative Indexing

AWS Elemental MediaTailor uniquely indexes each creative by the value of the `id` attribute provided in the `<Creative>` element. If a creative's ID is not specified, AWS Elemental MediaTailor uses the media file URL for the index.

The following example declaration shows the creative ID:

```
1 <Creatives>
2    <Creative id="57859154776" sequence="1">
```

If you define your own creative IDs, use a new, unique ID for each creative. Do not reuse creative IDs. AWS Elemental MediaTailor stores creative content for repeated use, and finds each by its indexed ID. When a new creative comes in, the service first checks its ID against the index. If the ID is present, AWS Elemental MediaTailor uses the stored content, rather than reprocessing the incoming content. If you reuse a creative ID, AWS Elemental MediaTailor uses the older, stored ad and does not play your new ad.

VPAID Handling

VPAID allows publishers to serve highly interactive video ads and to provide viewability metrics on their monetized streams. For information about VPAID, see the specification at https://www.iab.com/guidelines/digital-video-player-ad-interface-definition-vpaid-2-0/.

AWS Elemental MediaTailor supports a mix of server-side-stitched VAST MP4 linear ads and client-side-inserted VPAID interactive creatives in the same ad break and preserves the order in which they appear in the VAST response. AWS Elemental MediaTailor follows VPAID redirects through a maximum of three levels of wrappers. The client-side reporting response includes the unwrapped VPAID metadata.

Follow these guidelines to use VPAID:

- Configure an MP4 slate for your VPAID creatives. AWS Elemental MediaTailor fills the VPAID ad slots with your configured slate, and provides VPAID ad metadata that is used on the client side to run the interactive ads. If you do not have a slate configured, when a VPAID ad appears, AWS Elemental MediaTailor logs an error in CloudWatch. It inserts MP4 ads normally no matter what. For more information, see Slate Management and Creating a Configuration.

- Use client-side reporting. AWS Elemental MediaTailor supports VPAID through our client-side reporting API. For more information, see Client-side Reporting.

  It is theoretically possible to use the default server-side reporting mode with VPAID. However, if you use server-side reporting, you lose any information about the presence of the VPAID ad and the metadata surrounding it, because that is only available through the client-side API.

- In live scenarios, make sure that your ad breaks, denoted by `EXT-X-CUE-OUT: Duration`, are large enough to accommodate any user interactivity on VPAID. For example, if the VAST XML specifies a VPAID ad that is 30 seconds long, implement your ad break to be more than 30 seconds, to accommodate the ad. If you don't do this, you lose the VPAID metadata, because the remaining duration in the ad break is not long enough to accommodate the VPAID ad.

Dynamic Ad Variables in AWS Elemental MediaTailor

The AWS Elemental MediaTailor request to the ad decision server (ADS) carries information about the current viewing session. Use query parameters in the ADS request URL to convey this information and to help the ADS configure an appropriate response to the AWS Elemental MediaTailor request. Parameters take the following forms:

- Static – values do not change from one session to the next. Static parameters typically capture information such as the response type that AWS Elemental MediaTailor expects from the ADS.

- Dynamic from AWS Elemental MediaTailor (session data) – AWS Elemental MediaTailor supplies unique parameter values for each session. The session ID is a common dynamic variable that AWS Elemental MediaTailor provides.

- Dynamic from the player (player data) – the player supplies unique parameter values for each session. Player-supplied values describe the viewer and help the ADS to determine which ads AWS Elemental MediaTailor stitches into the stream.

To pass session and player information to the ADS

1. Work with the ADS to determine the information that it needs to respond to an ad query from AWS Elemental MediaTailor.

2. Create a configuration in AWS Elemental MediaTailor using a template ADS request URL that includes static parameters and placeholders for dynamic parameters. Session data is represented in `session` parameters, and player data is represented in `player_params` parameters. Use this template URL in the AWS Elemental MediaTailor **Ad decision server** field.
   Example

   In the following example, `correlation` is session data (the session ID), and `user` is player data (the user ID):

   1 `https://my.ads.server.com/path?correlation=[session.id]&user=[player_params.userID]`

3. Configure the request to AWS Elemental MediaTailor from the player to include the necessary player data. To identify the parameters for the ADS, use the `ads.` prefix before all ADS information. AWS Elemental MediaTailor passes any variables that are not preceded with `ads.` to the origin server.

   Include parameters in the session initiation request only. They're not needed in subsequent requests to AWS Elemental MediaTailor for this session.
   Example

   In the following example request to AWS Elemental MediaTailor, `userID` goes to the ADS and `auth_token` goes to the origin server:

   1 `GET master.m3u8?ads.userID=xyzuser&auth_token=kjhdsaf7gh`

4. When the player initiates a session, AWS Elemental MediaTailor replaces the variables in the template ADS request URL with session and player data. The remaining parameters are passed to the origin server.
   Example

   In the following examples, session and player data is sent to the ADS. The authorization token is sent to the origin server:

   1 `https://my.ads.server.com/path?correlation=896976764&user=xyzuser`

   1 `https://my.origin.server.com/master.m3u8?auth_token=kjhdsaf7gh`

The following sections describe how to configure session and player data.

- Session Data
- Player Data

Session Data

AWS Elemental MediaTailor generates data about each playback session. AWS Elemental MediaTailor replaces the `session` and `avail` query parameters in the template ADS request URL with this data when making a request to the ADS. You can also concatenate multiple variables together to achieve the value that you want.

You can use the following variables in the template ADS request URL:

- **[session.id]** – unique numeric identifier for the current playback session. All requests that a player makes during a session have the same value for this field, so it can be used for ADS fields that are intended to correlate requests for a single viewing.

- **[session.uuid]** – alternative to **[session.id]**. This is a unique identifier for the current playback session, such as the following:

```
1  e039fd39-09f0-46b2-aca9-9871cc116cde
```

- **[session.referer]** – usually, the URL of the page that is hosting the video player. This variable is set to the value of the `Referer` header that the player uses in its request to AWS Elemental MediaTailor. If the player doesn't include this header, the **[session.referer]** value is empty. If you're using a CDN or proxy in front of the manifest endpoint, you must proxy the correct header from the player here.

- **[session.user_agent]** – the `User-Agent` header that AWS Elemental MediaTailor received from the player's session initialization request. If you're using a CDN or proxy in front of the manifest endpoint, you must proxy the correct header from the player here.

- **[session.client_ip]** – the remote IP address that the AWS Elemental MediaTailor request came from. If the `X-forwarded-for` header is set, then that value is what AWS Elemental MediaTailor uses for the `client_ip`.

- **[session.avail_duration_secs]** – the duration in seconds of the ad availability slot that is being requested. AWS Elemental MediaTailor obtains the duration value from the input manifest's `#EXT-X-CUE-OUT: DURATION` or from values in the `#EXT-X-DATERANGE` tag. If the input manifest has a null, invalid, or 0 duration for the ad break in those tags, AWS Elemental MediaTailor uses a default value of 300 seconds.

- **[session.avail_duration_ms]** – the duration in milliseconds of the ad availability slot that is being requested. AWS Elemental MediaTailor obtains the duration value from the input manifest's `#EXT-X-CUE-OUT: DURATION` or from values in the `#EXT-X-DATERANGE` tag. If the input manifest has a null, invalid, or 0 duration for the ad break in those tags, AWS Elemental MediaTailor uses a default value of 300,000 ms.

- **[avail.random]** – a random number between 0 and 10000000000 that AWS Elemental MediaTailor generates for each request to the ADS. Some ad servers use this parameter to enable features such as separating ads from competing companies.

- **[avail_num]** – the value parsed from the SCTE-35 field `avail_num`. AWS Elemental MediaTailor can use this value to designate linear ad break numbers.

Example
If the ADS requires a query parameter named `deviceSession` to be passed with the unique session identifier, the template ADS URL in AWS Elemental MediaTailor could look like the following:

```
1  https://my.ads.server.com/path?deviceSession=[session.id]
```

AWS Elemental MediaTailor automatically generates a unique identifier for each stream, and enters the identifier in place of `session.id`. If the identifier is 1234567, the final request that AWS Elemental MediaTailor makes to the ADS would look something like this:

```
1  https://my.ads.server.com/path?deviceSession=1234567
```

Player Data

To send data from the player to the ADS, use `player_params.<query_parameter_name>` variables in the template ADS URL. For example, if the player sends a query parameter named `user_id` in its request to AWS Elemental MediaTailor and you need to pass that data in the ADS request, then include `[player_params. user_id]` anywhere in the ADS URL configuration.

When AWS Elemental MediaTailor receives a manifest request from the player, it URL-decodes the values of the query parameters in the player request once and substitutes the values of the parameters into the variables in the ADS request URL. If your ADS is expecting a URL-encoded value as the query parameter (instead of a URL-decoded value), then you must URL-encode the value from the player twice.

This functionality allows you to control the query parameters that are included in the ADS request. The most common methods of control are as follows:

- Dynamically adding query parameters to the ADS request

- Passing arbitrary key-value pairs as the value of a special query parameter that your ADS recognizes

The following sections provide more information about these methods.

Adding Query Parameters

To take data from a query parameter provided by the player and include it as a query parameter in the ADS request, do the following:

1. URL-encode the key-value pairs on the player.

2. Pass the pairs to AWS Elemental MediaTailor as the value of a single query parameter.

3. Reference the player parameter in the ADS request URL configuration.

The following example shows how this is done.

Note
For client-side reporting, you don't need to URL-encode query strings in the JSON object of the session initiation request. Query strings are passed through as-is from the JSON object.

Pairs:

- *param1* with a value of *value1:*

- *param2* with a value of *value2:*

To add query parameters

1. URL-encode the pairs.

   The decoded representation of the values that must be sent to the ADS is `param1=value1:&param2= value2:`, so the URL-encoded representation is `param1=value1%3A&param2=value2%3A`.

2. Pass the URL-encoded pairs to AWS Elemental MediaTailor.

   The request is some variation of the following:

```
1 <masterAssetID>.m3u8?ads.param1=value1%3A&ads.param2=value2%3A
```

3. In AWS Elemental MediaTailor, make sure the ADS request URL references the parameter, such as the following:

```
1 https://my.ads.com/path?param1=[player_params.param1]&param2=[player_params.param2]
```

4. AWS Elemental MediaTailor decodes the parameter when the player request is received. AWS Elemental MediaTailor sends the following request to the ADS:

```
1 https://my.ads.com/<path>?param1=value1:&param2=value2:
```

In this way, the `param1` and `param2` key-value pairs are included as first-class query parameters in the ADS request.

Advanced Usage

You can customize the ADS request in many ways with player parameterization. The only requirement is that the ADS hostname be included.

Customization examples:

- Concatenate player_params and session parameters to create new parameters. Example:

```
1 ?key1=[player_params.value1][session.id]
```

- Use a player parameter as part of a path element. Example:

```
1 https://my.ads.com/[player_params.path]?key=value
```

- Use player parameters to pass both path elements and keys themselves, rather than just values. Example:

```
1 https://my.ads.com/[player_params.path]?[player_params.key1]=[player_params.value1]
```

Ad Behavior in AWS Elemental MediaTailor

AWS Elemental MediaTailor can perform ad replacement (replace content segments with ad content) or ad insertion (insert ad content where segments don't currently exist). The ad behavior depends on the type of content (VOD or live), and how the origin server configured the ad breaks. Additionally, AWS Elemental MediaTailor uses configured slates to fill gaps in ads and manage VPAID ad handling.

Generally, the ad flow goes like this:

1. The player requests a master manifest from AWS Elemental MediaTailor.

2. AWS Elemental MediaTailor requests a VAST (or VMAP) response from the ad decision server (ADS) and master manifest from the origin server.

3. AWS Elemental MediaTailor stitches ads into the master manifest based on the response from the ADS.

   The following sections describe the logic that AWS Elemental MediaTailor uses when stitching ads into a manifest.

   - VOD Content Ad Behavior
   - Live Content Ad Behavior
   - Slate Management

VOD Content Ad Behavior

AWS Elemental MediaTailor inserts or replaces ads in VOD streams, based on how the origin server configured the CUE-OUT/CUE-IN (or SCTE-OUT/SCTE-IN) markers in the master manifest, or whether the ad decision server (ADS) sends VMAP responses.

For ad behavior by marker configuration, see the following sections.

- No XX-OUT/XX-IN Markers
- XX-OUT/XX-IN Markers Are Present

No XX-OUT/XX-IN Markers

Although CUE-OUT/IN (or SCTE-OUT/IN) markers are the preferred way of signaling ad breaks in a live manifest, the markers are not required for VOD content. If the manifest doesn't contain ad markers, AWS Elemental MediaTailor makes a single call to the ad decision server (ADS) and creates ad breaks based on the response:

- If the ADS sends a VAST response, then AWS Elemental MediaTailor inserts all ads from the response in an ad break at the start of the manifest. This is a pre-roll.

- If the ADS sends a VMAP response, then AWS Elemental MediaTailor uses the ad break time offsets to create breaks and insert them throughout the manifest at the specified times (pre-roll, mid-roll, or post-roll). AWS Elemental MediaTailor uses all ads from each ad break in the VMAP response for each ad break in the manifest. **Tip**
  If you want to create mid-roll breaks but your ADS doesn't support VMAP, then ensure that there are CUE-OUT (or SCTE-OUT) markers in the manifest. AWS Elemental MediaTailor inserts ads at the markers, as described in the following sections.

XX-OUT/XX-IN Markers Are Present

CUE-OUT/IN (or SCTE-OUT/IN) markers allow AWS Elemental MediaTailor to insert ads throughout the manifest. If the manifest contains markers, and the CUE-IN marker immediately follows the CUE-OUT marker (there are no segments between them), this informs AWS Elemental MediaTailor that it is an ad insertion request.

The CUE-OUT markers should have no duration (or a duration of 0) specified, such as `#EXT-X-CUE-OUT:0`.

For post-rolls, CUE-OUT/IN markers must precede the last content segment. This is because the HLS spec requires tag decorators to be explicitly declared before a segment.

For example, for the following declaration:

```
1 #EXT-X-CUE-OUT: 0
2 #EXT-X-CUE-IN
3 #EXTINF:4.000,
4 Videocontent.ts
5 #EXT-X-ENDLIST
```

AWS Elemental MediaTailor inserts a post-roll like the following:

```
1 #EXTINF:4.000,
2 Videocontent.ts
3 #EXT-X-DISCONTINUITY
4 #EXTINF:3.0,
5 Adsegment1.ts
6 #EXTINF:3.0,
7 Adsegment2.ts
```

51

```
 8 #EXTINF:1.0,
 9 Adsegment3.ts
10 #EXT-X-ENDLIST
```

You cannot use multiple CUE-OUT/IN tags in succession to mimic ad pod behavior. This is because CUE-OUT/IN tags must be explicitly attached to a segment.

For example, the following declaration is invalid:

```
 1 #EXT-X-CUE-OUT: 0
 2 #EXT-X-CUE-IN
 3 #EXT-X-CUE-OUT: 0
 4 #EXT-X-CUE-IN
 5 #EXT-X-CUE-OUT: 0
 6 #EXT-X-CUE-IN
 7 #EXTINF:4.000,
 8 Videocontent.ts
```

The following declaration is valid:

```
 1 #EXT-X-CUE-OUT: 0
 2 #EXT-X-CUE-IN
 3 #EXTINF:4.000,
 4 Somecontent1.ts
 5 #EXT-X-CUE-OUT: 0
 6 #EXT-X-CUE-IN
 7 #EXTINF:4.000,
 8 Somecontent2.ts
 9 #EXT-X-CUE-OUT: 0
10 #EXT-X-CUE-IN
11 #EXTINF:4.000,
12 Videocontent.ts
```

The above declaration results in an output like the following:

```
 1 Ad 1
 2 Somecontent.ts
 3 Ad 2
 4 Somecontent2.ts
 5 Videocontent.ts
 6 Post-Roll Ad 3
```

Live Content Ad Behavior

In live streams, AWS Elemental MediaTailor always performs ad replacement, with the total time between XX-OUT and XX-IN markers preserved as closely as possible. Note the following about live ad insertion:

- AWS Elemental MediaTailor always prioritizes the content stream over ad content. If AWS Elemental MediaTailor encounters an early CUE-IN before the ad break time has elapsed, the ad might be truncated.

- If there aren't enough ads in the VAST response to fill the ad break in the manifest, AWS Elemental MediaTailor plays the underlying stream (or the ad slate if one was provided in the ADS and origin server configuration).

- If the fragment duration for individual ads exceeds the ad break in the manifest, AWS Elemental MediaTailor fits as many complete ads as it can. When it can't fit any more complete ads, AWS Elemental MediaTailor plays the slate or underlying stream.

  If the ad break is for 70 seconds but the VAST response includes two ads, each of which is 40 seconds, AWS Elemental MediaTailor plays one ad for a total of 40 seconds and then displays the configured ad slate or underlying content stream for the remaining 30 seconds of the ad break.

Ad behavior is further refined by the length of the CUE-OUT duration, as described in the following sections.

XX-OUT Duration Greater Than Zero

If the CUE-OUT (or SCTE-OUT) duration is greater than zero, AWS Elemental MediaTailor replaces as many ads that fit in the ad break without truncation:

- If the VAST response includes a single ad and the ad break duration is less than the ad creative duration, AWS Elemental MediaTailor doesn't splice any ads into the content stream. Instead, the service displays the configured ad slate or underlying content stream for the duration of the break.

- If the CUE-IN is presented earlier than expected, AWS Elemental MediaTailor honors the CUE-IN and returns to the content stream, possibly cutting off some of the ad.

- If the CUE-IN is not encountered by the time the CUE-OUT duration is reached, AWS Elemental MediaTailor ends the ad break and the stream returns to the content stream.

XX-OUT Duration Equal to Zero

If the CUE-OUT (or SCTE-OUT) duration is zero, AWS Elemental MediaTailor splices in all ads from the ADS response until it encounters a CUE-IN marker. No CUE-IN markers in a live scenario is an error state that requires attention.

Slate Management

In AWS Elemental MediaTailor, you can configure a URL to an MP4 slate, to be used to fill gaps in media content. AWS Elemental MediaTailor inserts the slate into unfilled and partially filled ad breaks. AWS Elemental MediaTailor downloads the slate from the MP4 URL and transcodes it to the same renditions as your content, for smooth transitions between the two. The slate may be played in a loop if the duration of the remaining ad break allows for it.

Configuring a slate is optional in all situations except where VPAID is used:

- For non-VPAID situations, if you don't configure a slate, AWS Elemental MediaTailor handles unfilled and partially filled ad breaks by showing the underlying stream content.

- For VPAID, you must configure a slate. AWS Elemental MediaTailor inserts the slate for the duration of the VPAID ad, though in certain cases, to accommodate user interactivity, this duration may be slightly higher than the duration of the VPAID ad as reported by VAST. The video player then handles the VPAID ad based on the client-side reporting metadata that AWS Elemental MediaTailor returns. For information about client-side reporting, see Client-side Reporting. For information about VPAID, see VPAID Handling.

The slate that you configure must be a high-quality MP4 asset that contains both audio and video. Empty audio slates sometimes cause playback issues on some players.

AWS Elemental MediaTailor shows the slate for the following situations:

- To fill in time that's not fully used by an ad replacement

- If the ad isn't available

- If the ADS responds with a blank VAST or VMAP response

- For error conditions, such as ADS timeout

- If ads are longer than the live ad break window

AWS Elemental MediaTailor always shows the slate near the end of the ad break.

Ad Tracking Reporting in AWS Elemental MediaTailor

Beacons are sent to the ad server to track and report on how much of an ad that a viewer has watched. AWS Elemental MediaTailor provides server-side ad reporting (AWS Elemental MediaTailor tracks the ad and sends beacons) or client-side tracking (the client player tracks the ad and sends beacons). The type of reporting that is used in a playback session depends on the request that the player uses to initiate the session in AWS Elemental MediaTailor.

- Server-side Reporting
- Client-side Reporting

Server-side Reporting

AWS Elemental MediaTailor defaults to server-side reporting: the service sends reports to the ad tracking URL directly when the player requests an ad URL from the playlist manifest. After the player initializes a playback session with AWS Elemental MediaTailor, no further input is required from you or the player to perform server-side reporting. As ads are played back, AWS Elemental MediaTailor sends beacons to the ad server to report how much of the ad is viewed. Beacons track the start of an ad, ad progression in quartiles (first, midpoint, and third), and when an ad is viewed to completion.

To perform server-side ad reporting

1. From the player, initialize a new AWS Elemental MediaTailor playback session using a request in the following format:

```
1 GET <mediatailorURL>/v1/master/<hashed-account-ID>/<originID>/<assetID>?ads.<key-value-
    pairs>
```

   where `<key-value-pairs>` are the targeting parameters for ad tracking. For information about adding parameters to the request, see Adding Query Parameters.

2. AWS Elemental MediaTailor responds to the request with the master manifest URL. The master manifest includes URLs for the media playlists. Links for ad segment requests are embedded in the media playlists.

3. When the player requests playback from an ad segment URL (`/v1/segment` path), AWS Elemental MediaTailor sends the appropriate beacon (start, complete, and quartiles) to the ad server through the ad tracking URLs. At the same time, the service issues a redirect to the actual *.ts ad segment either in the Amazon CloudFront distribution where AWS Elemental MediaTailor stores transcoded ads, or in the content distribution network (CDN) where you have cached the ad.

   AWS Elemental MediaTailor sends a beacon each time a player makes a request to the `/v1/segment` URL. If the player has to make multiple requests to the same URL (in conditions such as network degradation), the service also sends multiple beacons. To avoid this duplication, use a CDN in front of AWS Elemental MediaTailor to cache the `/v1/segment` URL path (as described in Integrating AWS Elemental MediaTailor and a CDN), or consider client-side reporting (as described in Client-side Reporting).

Client-side Reporting

With client-side reporting, AWS Elemental MediaTailor proxies the ad tracking URL to the client player. The player then performs all ad-tracking activities. Client-side reporting enables functionality like trick play for VOD (players display visual feedback during fast forward and rewind) and other advanced playback behavior during ad breaks that requires player development (like no skip-forward and countdown timers on ad breaks).

Use client-side reporting for VPAID functionality. For more information, see VPAID Handling. The client-side reporting response includes additional metadata about the VPAID creative.

To perform client-side ad reporting

1. From the player, initialize a new AWS Elemental MediaTailor playback session using a request in the following JSON format:

```
1 POST <mediatailorURL>/v1/session/<hashed-account-ID>/<originID>/<assetID>
2     {
3
4         adsParams: {
5             param1: "value1",
6             param2: "value2",
7             param3: "value3",
8         }
9     }
```

   where:

   - `adsParams` are values that AWS Elemental MediaTailor has to use in the request to the ADS. Define the `adsParams` parameters as `[player_params.param]` in the ADS template URL in the AWS Elemental MediaTailor configuration, as described in Step 3: Configure ADS Request URL and Query Parameters.

   - any other query parameters are forwarded to your origin server.

2. AWS Elemental MediaTailor responds to the request with two URLs, one for the manifest and one for the tracking endpoint:

   - Manifest – used to retrieve content playlists and ad segments

     Example: `<mediatailorURL>/v1/master/<hashed-account-id>/<originID>/<assetID>?aws.sessionID=<session>`

   - Tracking – used to poll for upcoming ad breaks

     Example: `<mediatailorURL>/v1/tracking/<hashed-account-id>/<originID>/<assetID>/<session>`

3. The player should periodically poll the tracking URL. When an ad is coming, the AWS Elemental MediaTailor response to the player's request to the tracking URL contains a JSON object with the time offsets for the ad breaks. These offsets are relative to when the player initiated the session. You can use them when programming specific behaviors in the player, such as preventing the viewer from skipping past the ads. The response also includes duration, timing, and identification information.

   These are the values that can be included in the response:

   - `adID`: HLS sequence number associated with the beginning of this ad.

   - `duration`: length in ISO 8601 seconds format. The response includes durations for the entire ad break and for each ad and beacon (though beacon durations are always zero). For VPAID Handling, the duration conveyed is the MP4 slate duration. This duration is typically slightly larger than the XML duration conveyed in VAST due to transcoder and segment duration configurations. You can interpret this as the maximum amount of time that you have to entirely replace with a VPAID ad without incurring drift.

- **durationInSeconds**: length in seconds format. The response includes durations for the entire ad break and for each ad and beacon (though beacon durations are always zero).

- **startTime**: time position in ISO 8601 seconds format, relative to the beginning of the playback session. The response includes start times for the entire ad break and for each ad and beacon.

- **startTimeInSeconds**: time position in seconds format, relative to the beginning of the playback session. The response includes start times for the entire ad break and for each ad and beacon.

- **beaconUrls**: where each beacon is sent.

- **eventId**: HLS sequence number associated with the beacon.

- **eventType**: type of beacon.

- **availId**: HLS sequence number associated with the start of the ad break.

- **apiFramework**: Set to "VPAID". Tells the player this is a VPAID ad.

- **adParameters**: String of ad parameters from VAST VPAID, which AWS Elemental MediaTailor passes along to the player.

- **mediaFilesList**: Assets that the player needs to know about.

- **mediaFileUri**: URI that points to either an executable or video asset. Example: `"https://myad.com/ad/ad134/vpaid.js"`.

- **delivery**: Either "**progressive**" or "**streaming**", depending on the protocol.

- **mediaType**: Typically either JavaScript or Flash for executable assets.

- **width**: Width of the video asset.

- **height**: Height of the video asset.

- **bitrate**: Bit rate of the video asset. This is not typically included for an executable asset.

- **scalable**: Indicates whether to scale the video to other dimensions.

- **maintainAspectRatio**: Indicates whether to maintain the aspect ratio while scaling.

- **mezzanine**: Specifies a mezzanine MP4 asset, if the VPAID ad includes one. Example: `"https://gcdn.2mdn.net/videoplayback/id/itag/ck2/file/file.mp4"`.

Example responses:

```
1  {
2    "avails": [
3      {
4        "ads": [
5          {
6            "adId": "8104385",
7            "duration": "PT15.100000078S",
8            "durationInSeconds": 15.1,
9            "startTime": "PT17.817798612S",
10           "startTimeInSeconds": 17.817,
11           "trackingEvents": [
12       {
13             "beaconUrls": [
14               "http://<mediatailorELB>/tracking?event=impression"
15             ],
16             "duration": "PT15.100000078S",
```

```
        "durationInSeconds": 15.1,
        "eventId": "8104385",
        "eventType": "impression",
        "startTime": "PT17.817798612S",
        "startTimeInSeconds": 17.817
    },
    {
        "beaconUrls": [
            "http://<mediatailorELB>/tracking?event=start"
        ],
        "duration": "PT0S",
        "durationInSeconds": 0.0,
        "eventId": "8104385",
        "eventType": "start",
        "startTime": "PT17.817798612S",
        "startTimeInSeconds": 17.817
    },
    {
        "beaconUrls": [
            "http://<mediatailorELB>/tracking?event=firstQuartile"
        ],
        "duration": "PT0S",
        "durationInSeconds": 0.0,
        "eventId": "8104386",
        "eventType": "firstQuartile",
        "startTime": "PT21.592798631S",
        "startTimeInSeconds": 21.592
    },
    {
        "beaconUrls": [
            "http://<mediatailorELB>/tracking?event=midpoint"
        ],
        "duration": "PT0S",
        "durationInSeconds": 0.0,
        "eventId": "8104387",
        "eventType": "midpoint",
        "startTime": "PT25.367798651S",
        "startTimeInSeconds": 25.367
    },
    {
        "beaconUrls": [
            "http://<mediatailorELB>/tracking?event=thirdQuartile"
        ],
        "duration": "PT0S",
        "durationInSeconds": 0.0,
        "eventId": "8104388",
        "eventType": "thirdQuartile",
        "startTime": "PT29.14279867S",
        "startTimeInSeconds": 29.142
    },
    {
        "beaconUrls": [
            "http://<mediatailorELB>/tracking?event=complete"
        ],
```

```
71            "duration": "PT0S",
72            "durationInSeconds": 0.0,
73            "eventId": "8104390",
74            "eventType": "complete",
75            "startTime": "PT32.91779869S",
76            "startTimeInSeconds": 32.917
77          }
78        ]
79      }
80    ],
81    "availId": "8104385",
82    "duration": "PT15.100000078S",
83    "durationInSeconds": 15.1,
84    "meta": null,
85    "startTime": "PT17.817798612S",
86    "startTimeInSeconds": 17.817
87  }
88  ]
89 }

1 {
2   "avails": [
3     {
4       "ads": [
5         {
6           "adId": "6744037",
7           "mediaFiles": {
8             "mezzanine": "https://gcdn.2mdn.net/videoplayback/id/itag/ck2/file/file.mp4",
9             "mediaFilesList": [
10              {
11                "mediaFileUri": "https://myad.com/ad/ad134/vpaid.js",
12                "delivery": "progressive",
13                "width": 176,
14                "height": 144,
15                "mediaType": "application/javascript",
16                "scalable": false,
17                "maintainAspectRatio": false,
18                "apiFramework": "VPAID"
19              },
20              {
21                "mediaFileUri": "https://myad.com/ad/ad134/file.mp4",
22                "delivery": "progressive",
23                "width": 640,
24                "height": 360,
25                "mediaType": "video/mp4",
26                "scalable": false,
27                "maintainAspectRatio": false
28              },
29              ...
30            ],
31            "adParameters": "[{'ads':[{"url":"https://myads/html5/media/LinearVPAIDCreative
               .mp4","mimetype":"video/mp4"}]}]",
32            "duration": "PT15.066667079S",
33            "durationInSeconds": 15.066,
34            "startTime": "PT39.700000165S",
```

60

```
35          "startTimeInSeconds": 39.7,
36          "trackingEvents": [
37            {
38              "beaconUrls": [
39                "https://beaconURL.com"
40              ],
41              "duration": "PT15.066667079S",
42              "durationInSeconds": 15.066,
43              "eventId": "6744037",
44              "eventType": "impression",
45              "startTime": "PT39.700000165S",
46              "startTimeInSeconds": 39.7
47            },
48            ...
49          ]
50        }
51      },
52      ...
53    ],
54    "availId": "6744037",
55    "duration": "PT45.166667157S",
56    "durationInSeconds": 45.166,
57    "meta": null,
58    "startTime": "PT39.700000165S",
59    "startTimeInSeconds": 39.7
60  }
61 ]
62 }
```

Monitoring and Troubleshooting AWS Elemental MediaTailor

Monitoring is an important part of maintaining the reliability, availability, and performance of AWS Elemental MediaTailor and your other AWS solutions. AWS provides the following monitoring tools to watch AWS Elemental MediaTailor, report when something is wrong, and take automatic actions when appropriate:

- *Amazon CloudWatch* monitors your AWS resources and the applications that you run on AWS in real time. You can collect and track metrics, create customized dashboards, and set alarms that notify you or take actions when a specified metric reaches a threshold that you specify. For example, you can have CloudWatch track CPU usage or other metrics of your Amazon EC2 instances and automatically launch new instances when needed. For more information, see the Amazon CloudWatch User Guide.

- *Amazon CloudWatch Logs* enables you to monitor, store, and access your log files from all interactions with your ad decision server (ADS). AWS Elemental MediaTailor emits logs for ad requests, redirects, responses, and reporting requests and responses. Errors from the ADS and origin servers are also emitted to log groups in Amazon CloudWatch. You can also archive your log data in highly durable storage. For more information, see the Amazon CloudWatch Logs User Guide.

- Setting up Permissions for Amazon CloudWatch

- Monitoring AWS Elemental MediaTailor with Amazon CloudWatch

Setting up Permissions for Amazon CloudWatch

Use AWS Identity and Access Management (IAM) to create a role that gives AWS Elemental MediaTailor access to Amazon CloudWatch. You must perform these steps for CloudWatch Logs to be published for your account. CloudWatch automatically publishes metrics for your account.

To allow AWS Elemental MediaTailor access to CloudWatch

1. Open the IAM console at https://console.aws.amazon.com/iam/.

2. In the navigation pane of the IAM console, choose **Roles**, and then choose **Create role**.

3. Choose the **Another AWS account** role type.

4. For **Account ID**, type your AWS account ID.

5. Select **Require external ID** and type **Midas**. This option automatically adds a condition to the trust policy that allows the service to assume the role only if the request includes the correct `sts:ExternalID`.

6. Choose **Next: Permissions**.

7. Add a permissions policy that specifies what actions this role can complete. Select from one of the following options, and then choose **Next: Review**:

   - **CloudWatchLogsFullAccess** to provide full access to Amazon CloudWatch Logs

   - **CloudWatchFullAccess** to provide full access to Amazon CloudWatch

8. For **Role name**, type **MediaTailorLogger**, and then choose **Create role**.

9. On the **Roles** page, choose the role that you just created.

10. To update the principal, edit the trust relationship:

    1. On the role's **Summary** page, choose the **Trust relationship** tab.

    2. Choose **Edit trust relationship**.

    3. In the policy document, change the principal to the AWS Elemental MediaTailor service. It should look like this:

    ```
    1 "Principal": {
    2     "Service": "mediatailor.amazonaws.com"
    3 },
    ```

    The entire policy should read as follows:

    ```
    1  {
    2    "Version": "2012-10-17",
    3    "Statement": [
    4      {
    5        "Effect": "Allow",
    6        "Principal": {
    7          "Service": "mediatailor.amazonaws.com"
    8        },
    9        "Action": "sts:AssumeRole",
    10       "Condition": {
    11         "StringEquals": {
    12           "sts:ExternalId": "Midas"
    13         }
    14       }
    15     }
    16   ]
    ```

```
17 }
```

4. Choose **Update Trust Policy**.

Monitoring AWS Elemental MediaTailor with Amazon CloudWatch

You can monitor AWS Elemental MediaTailor using CloudWatch, which collects raw data and processes it into readable, near real-time metrics. These statistics are kept for 15 months, so that you can access historical information and gain a better perspective on how your web application or service is performing. You can also set alarms that watch for certain thresholds, and send notifications or take actions when those thresholds are met. For more information, see the Amazon CloudWatch User Guide.

To view metrics using the CloudWatch console

Metrics are grouped first by the service namespace, and then by the various dimension combinations within each namespace.

1. Open the CloudWatch console at https://console.aws.amazon.com/cloudwatch/.

2. In the navigation pane, choose **Metrics**.

3. Under **All metrics**, choose the **MediaTailor** namespace.

4. Select the metric dimension to view the metrics (for example, originID).

To view metrics using the AWS CLI

At a command prompt, use the following command.

```
1 aws cloudwatch list-metrics --namespace "AWS/MediaTailor"
```

AWS Elemental MediaTailor CloudWatch Metrics

The MediaTailor namespace includes the following metrics. These metrics are published by default to your account.

Metric	Description
AdDecisionServer.Ads	Count of ads included in ad decision server (ADS) responses for the time period that you specified.
AdDecisionServer.Duration	Total duration (in milliseconds) of all ads that AWS Elemental MediaTailor received from the ad decision server (ADS) in the time period that you specified.
AdDecisionServer.Errors	Number of non-HTTP 200 status code responses or empty responses that AWS Elemental MediaTailor received from the ad decision server (ADS) in the time period that you specified.

Metric	Description
AdDecisionServer.FillRate	The simple average of the rate that responses from the ad decision server (ADS) were filled. The rate is defined as (AdDecisionServer.Duration)/(Avails.Duration). This number can be higher than 100%.**Example 1**If your ADS returns 120 seconds of ads and the ad break is 180 seconds, then the`AdDecisionServer.FillRate` is 67% (120/180). The best `Avails.FillRate` that we can attain for this ad break is therefore 67%.**Example 2**If your ADS returns 120 seconds of ads and the ad break is 90 seconds, then the `AdDecisionServer.FillRate` is 133% (120/90). The best `Avails.FillRate` that we can attain for this ad break is therefore 100%.For information about the simple average, see Simple Average Explanation.
AdNotReady	Number of times that the ADS pointed at an ad that wasn't yet transcoded by the internal transcoder service. A high incidence of this metric might contribute to a low overall `Avails.FillRate`.
Avails.Duration	Total duration (in milliseconds) of all ad breaks that AWS Elemental MediaTailor encountered in the time period that you specified.
Avails.FilledDuration	Total duration (in milliseconds) of all ad breaks that AWS Elemental MediaTailor filled in the time period that you specified.This metric is calculated as (number of concurrent sessions) x (ad break duration filled).
Avails.FillRate	The simple average of the rate that ad breaks were filled. The rate is defined as (`Avails.FilledDuration`) / (`Avails.Duration`). For information about the simple average, see Simple Average Explanation. **Example** If your ADS returns 90 seconds of ads and the ad break is 120 seconds, then the `AdDecisionServer.FillRate` is 75% (90/120). If the `Avails.FillRate` is low, look at the `AdDecisionServer.FillRate` compared to the `Avails.FillRate`. If the `AdDecisionServer.FillRate` is low (50% or lower) and `Avails.FillRate` is also low, your ADS might be returning only enough ads for half of a typical break duration, so the maximum `Avails.FillRate` that we can attain is bounded by 50%.
GetManifest.Errors	Number of errors received when AWS Elemental MediaTailor is generating manifests.

Metric	Description
Origin.Errors	Number of non-HTTP 200 status code responses that AWS Elemental MediaTailor received from the origin server in the time period that you specified.

Simple Average Explanation

Simple average means that the durations aren't weighted in the FillRate calculation. The FillRate for each ad break is simply averaged together. This gives an overall view of how successful ad insertions are across all of your ad breaks, independent of how long each ad break is. To get a weighted average, calculate the sum of your **total duration** and divide by the **total filled duration** in a time period.

Example

You have the following two ad breaks:

- Ad break A: 90 seconds total duration, 45 seconds filled (50% filled)
- Ad break B: 120 seconds total duration, 120 seconds filled (100% filled)

The FillRate metric reported is 75% ([50% + 100%] / 2).

The actual weighted average FillRate is 79% ([45 seconds filled + 120 seconds filled] / [90 total seconds + 120 total seconds]).

AWS Elemental MediaTailor CloudWatch Dimensions

You can filter the AWS Elemental MediaTailor data using the following dimensions.

Dimension	Description
Configuration Name	Indicates the configuration that the metric belongs to.

Limits in AWS Elemental MediaTailor

The following sections provide information about the limits in AWS Elemental MediaTailor. For information about requesting an increase to soft limits, see AWS Service Limits. Hard limits cannot be changed.

Soft Limits

The following table describes limits in AWS Elemental MediaTailor that can be increased. For information about changing limits, see AWS Service Limits.

Resource or Operation	Default Limit
Transactions	3,000 concurrent transactions per second across all request types (such as manifest requests and tracking requests for client-side reporting). This is an account-level limit. Your transactions per second are largely dependent on how often the player requests updated manifests. For example, a player with eight second segments might update the manifest every eight seconds. The player, then, generates 0.125 transactions per second. To request a limit increase, create a case with AWS Support.

Hard Limits

The following table describes limits within AWS Elemental MediaTailor that can't be increased.

Resource or Operation	Default Limit
Configurations	50
Characters per field	Content origin: 512 **Ad decision server:** 25,000
Ad decision server (ADS) timeout	AWS Elemental MediaTailor waits for 1.5 seconds before timing out on an open connection to an ad server. When a connection times out, AWS Elemental MediaTailor is unable to fill the ad break with ads due to no response from the ADS.
Origin server timeout	AWS Elemental MediaTailor waits for two seconds before timing out on an open connection to the origin server when requesting template manifests. Timeouts generate HTTP 504 (Gateway Time-out) response errors.
ADS redirect	AWS Elemental MediaTailor follows a maximum of three redirects in VAST wrapper tags.

Resource or Operation	Default Limit
Sessions becoming stale	Sessions expire after 10 times the manifest duration if there are no requests during that timeframe, or if the origin server does not advance in that timeframe. For example, if a manifest has one minute's worth of segments, the player must make a request or the origin server must advance within 10 minutes. Otherwise, AWS Elemental MediaTailor starts returning HTTP 400 (Bad Request) response errors (bad request for expired sessions).
Manifest size	The size of any playback manifest, input or output, is limited to a maximum of 1 MB. Please gzip your input manifest into AWS Elemental MediaTailor to ensure that you stay under this limit.

AWS Elemental MediaTailor Resources

The following table lists related resources that you'll find useful as you work with AWS Elemental MediaTailor.

Resource	Description
Classes and Workshops	Links to role-based and specialty courses as well as self-paced labs to help sharpen your AWS skills and gain practical experience.
AWS Developer Tools	Links to developer tools, SDKs, IDE tool kits, and command line tools for developing and managing AWS applications.
AWS Whitepapers	Links to a comprehensive list of technical AWS whitepapers, covering topics such as architecture, security, and economics and authored by AWS Solutions Architects or other technical experts.
AWS Support Center	The hub for creating and managing your AWS Support cases. Also includes links to other helpful resources, such as forums, technical FAQs, service health status, and AWS Trusted Advisor.
https://aws.amazon.com/premiumsupport/	The primary webpage for information about AWS Support, a one-on-one, fast-response support channel to help you build and run applications in the cloud.
Contact Us	A central contact point for inquiries concerning AWS billing, account, events, abuse, and other issues.
AWS Site Terms	Detailed information about our copyright and trademark; your account, license, and site access; and other topics.

Document History for AWS Elemental MediaTailor

The following table describes important changes to this documentation.

- **API version:** 1.0

Change	Description	Date
Add information for Cloud-Watch and for VAST/VPAID.	Added information about available CloudWatch metrics, namespaces, and dimensions in Monitoring and Troubleshooting AWS Elemental MediaTailor. Added and updated information for VAST and VPAID in VAST, Client-side Reporting and Slate Management.	March 16, 2018
Enable github delivery.	Open source delivery of public documentation assets.	February 16, 2018
Added new regions.	In Regions for AWS Elemental MediaTailor, added Singapore, Sydney, and Tokyo.	February 8, 2018
Added default Amazon Cloud-Front distribution paths for ad storage.	In Integrating AWS Elemental MediaTailor and a CDN, added the list of paths for the Amazon CloudFront distributions where AWS Elemental MediaTailor stores ads.	February 6, 2018
Added IAM policy information specific to AWS Elemental MediaTailor.	In Setting Up AWS Elemental MediaTailor, added instructions for creating non-admin roles with limited permissions.	January 3, 2018
Added default Amazon Cloud-Front distribution paths for ad storage.	In Integrating AWS Elemental MediaTailor and a CDN, added the list of paths for the Amazon CloudFront distributions where AWS Elemental MediaTailor stores ads.	January 26, 2018

Note
The AWS Media Services are not designed or intended for use with applications or in situations requiring fail-safe performance, such as life safety operations, navigation or communication systems, air traffic control, or life support machines in which the unavailability, interruption or failure of the services could lead to death, personal injury, property damage or environmental damage.

AWS Glossary

For the latest AWS terminology, see the AWS Glossary in the *AWS General Reference*.

www.ingramcontent.com/pod-product-compliance
Lightning Source LLC
LaVergne TN
LVHW082041050326
832904LV00005B/267